KT-512-158

FIND OUT ABOUT

weather

Terry Jennings

BBC

© **Terry Jennings / BBC Education 1998**

BBC Education
201 Wood Lane
London W12 7TS

ISBN 0 563 37382 2

Editor: Christina Digby
Designer: Charlotte Crace
Picture research: Helen Taylor
Educational advisers: Samina Miller, Shelagh Scarborough
Photographers: Simon Pugh, Lesley Howling (child on front cover)
Illustrator: Line & Line

With grateful thanks to: Felina Tramonti; Kathryn Earl; Dr John Green, UEA;
Graham Butler, National Meteorological Office

Researched photographs ©: Bruce Coleman Collection (page 14 top right, 16 detail);
ESA/D Parker (page 22 detail); Robert Harding Picture Library (pages 9 left, 11 left, 14
bottom right, 17 left); Images Colour Library (pages 5, 7, 15 and 16); NHPA (pages 18
and 21); Oxford Scientific Films (page 11 right); Panos Pictures (page 9 right); Planet
Earth Pictures (page 14 top left); Science Photo Library (pages 14 bottom left, 17 right,
19, 20 and 22)

Origination by Goodfellow & Egan, Peterborough
Printed in Belgium by Proost

Contents

We wear different clothes to suit the weather. What is the weather like where these children are? How can you tell?

What is the weather like where you are today? What are you wearing?

What is weather?

Weather is what we see or feel outside every day. In most parts of the world the weather changes all the time. Some days it feels hot. Some days it feels cold. Some days it rains, other days are dry. Some days are sunny, other days are cloudy and dull. Sometimes the wind blows. Other days the air is still. These are some of the changes that make up our weather.

The heat of the sun makes all our weather. The sun shines all the time, but we cannot always see it if there are clouds in the sky. Clouds block out some of the sunlight.

It is usually **cold** in **winter**.

It is usually **warm** in **summer**.

body temperature

What **temperature** does this **thermometer** show?

We measure **temperature** in **degrees Celsius**. Each mark on this **thermometer** is one degree Celsius.

water freezes at 0°C

What is temperature?

The sun can make us feel hot in summer. Then we wear thin light clothes. On some sunny days the wind can make us feel cold. We may also feel cold when it is raining. In winter it can be very cold. If we go out we need to put on warm clothes.

Temperature is a measure of how hot or cold the weather is. A thermometer is used to measure the temperature. It shows the temperature in degrees. Each mark on the thermometer is one degree Celsius. We write it as 1°C.

The **hottest** days are in **summer** when there are no **clouds** in the sky.

You can fly a kite in the **wind**. The **wind** helps the kite to stay up high.

the **sun** warms the land

cool air comes in as **wind**

warm air rising from land

Why does the wind blow?

We cannot see the wind. We feel it when it blows against us. The wind can be gentle or it can be strong. When the wind blows gently through the trees, we can hear the leaves rustling. It is hard to walk or run in a very strong wind. The trees sway in a strong wind. Very strong winds may damage houses and uproot trees.

Wind is moving air. Winds blow because the sun warms some parts of the Earth more than others. The warm parts of the Earth warm the air above them. The warm air rises and cold air comes in to take its place. As the air moves from one place to another it makes a wind.

The strongest wind is called a **hurricane**. It can destroy houses and uproot trees.

We can use wind to sail boats.

sun

clouds

rain

river

water vapour

sea

Rain collects in the sea, streams, rivers and lakes.

Where does rain come from?

Rain makes puddles of water on the ground. The sun soon dries up the puddles. The water in the puddles turns into an invisible gas called water vapour. The water vapour rises into the air.

The sun shining on the sea turns water to vapour all the time. When the vapour cools in the sky, it makes clouds. Clouds are made of millions of little drops of water. The drops are so small and light that they stay up in the air. Sometimes the tiny drops bump into each other. They join to form bigger drops. These fall to the ground as rain.

If it rains for a long time we may have **floods**.

If it doesn't rain for a long time we have a **drought**.

Make a **wind wheel** to see how hard the wind is blowing.

Make a pin-hole in the middle of a paper plate.

Paint a paper cup.

Tape four paper cups to the plate.

Using a drawing pin, fasten the paper plate to the top of a stick. See that the plate turns easily.

Take your wind wheel outside each morning. The harder the wind blows, the faster the wheel will turn.

Using a timer, count how many times it turns in one minute.

How can we measure the wind and rain?

You can collect rain to see how much has fallen. Ask an adult to cut the top off a plastic bottle. Stand this rain collector out in the open. Put bricks around it so that it doesn't fall over.

Every morning look at your rain collector to see how much rain has fallen. Pour each day's rain into a little bottle. Use a new bottle each day. All the bottles must be the same. Label the bottles. Use a ruler to measure how much rain has fallen. On which day did most rain fall? Which days were dry? How much water fell in a week?

plastic bottle with top cut off

rain collects in bottle

small bottles

stratus clouds

cirrus clouds

cumulus clouds

thunder clouds

What is a cloud?

Clouds are made up of tiny droplets of water or pieces of ice floating in the air. There are three main kinds of cloud.

Stratus is a low, grey blanket of cloud. Often stratus clouds bring drizzle.

Cirrus clouds are thin wisps of cloud, high in the sky. Often they show that warmer weather is coming.

Cumulus clouds look like giant puffs of cotton wool. We see them on warm, sunny days. When cumulus clouds grow very tall, rain or a thunderstorm may follow.

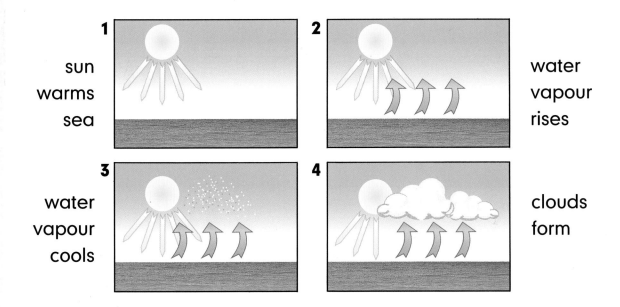

1   sun warms sea

2   water vapour rises

3   water vapour cools

4   clouds form

These little drops of water on a piece of grass are **dew.**

How far can you see through the **mist?**

What are dew, mist and fog?

Some mornings the grass is wet, although it hasn't rained. The little drops of water are called dew. At night some of the water vapour in the air cools and turns to little drops of water. It forms dew on grass, the ground and cars.

When clouds come down to the ground, we have mist or fog. Both are made up of tiny droplets of water. We can see quite a long way when it is misty. It is very hard to see when it is foggy.

Many cities have smog, a mixture of smoke and fog.

It is hard to see when it is **foggy**.

Smog can make it difficult to **breathe**.

Ice floats on top of the **water** in a pond, so the fish can go on living in the water underneath.

What are snow, ice and frost?

If the weather is very cold, the tiny drops of water in the clouds turn to ice. Each piece of ice is a shape called a crystal. The ice crystals grow then fall as snowflakes.

When the weather is very cold, water on the ground freezes. It turns to ice. The water in ponds may freeze. Ice floats on water and so ponds have ice on top of them.

Sometimes on very cold nights the water vapour in the air freezes. It turns to little drops of ice. Everything is then covered with the tiny white crystals we call frost. Frost often makes beautiful patterns on windows.

Every **snowflake** has six sides. No one has ever found two snowflakes exactly the same.

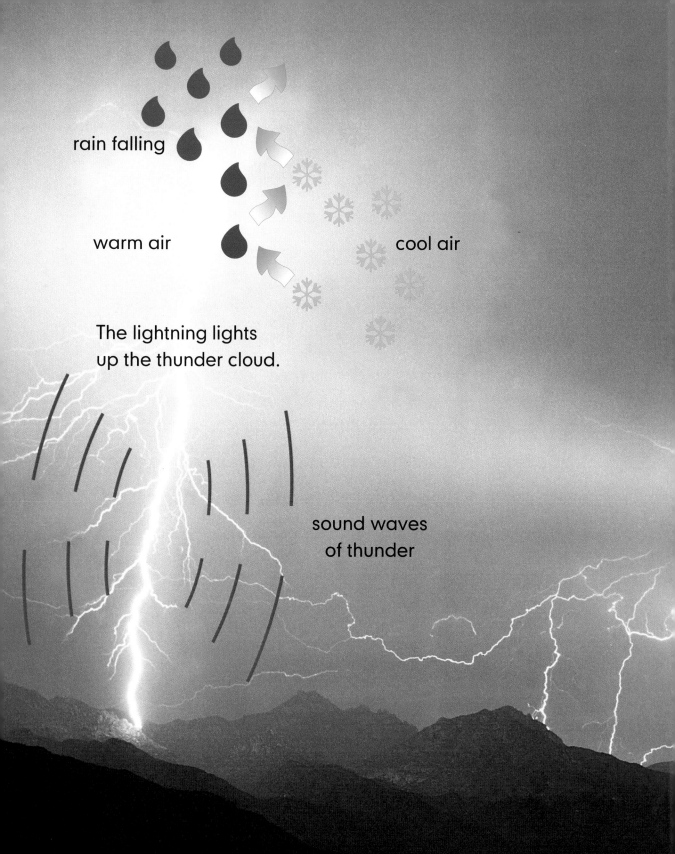

rain falling

warm air

cool air

The lightning lights
up the thunder cloud.

sound waves
of thunder

Why do we have thunderstorms?

Thunderstorms happen when huge amounts of warm, moist air rise quickly. The clouds grow tall and dark. Inside the clouds drops of water going down bang into pieces of ice going up. This makes electricity. It escapes to the ground as a huge spark. The lightning heats the air around it. This makes the loud noise of thunder.

Sometimes hail falls. Hailstones are frozen raindrops. Most are small like peas. Some are as big as apples.

Lightning can damage buildings and injure or kill people. It often strikes tall trees, so do not shelter under them.

This tree has been struck by **lightning**.

Weather satellites are sent out to space. **Cameras** inside
the satellite take photographs of the Earth and the clouds.
Thermometers measure the **temperature** of the air.
All the information is sent to Earth, to help people make
weather maps.

What will the weather be like?

We like to know what the weather is going to be. We might want to go on a picnic or to play outside. We might want to go to the sea if it is going to be hot and sunny.

Scientists who forecast the weather use special instruments. They use large balloons to collect information about the air high in the sky. They use satellites out in space to take photographs of the weather all over the world. People make maps to show what is happening to the weather. They use special symbols to show the sun, clouds and rain.

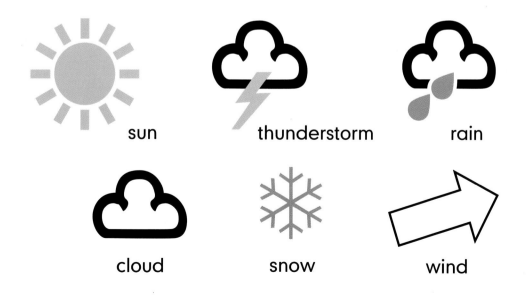

sun   thunderstorm   rain

cloud   snow   wind

Index

~~~~~~~~